The Concise Illustrated Book of
Modern Sports Cars

Laurie Ward

GALLERY BOOKS
An imprint of W. H. Smith Publishers Inc.
112 Madison Avenue
New York, New York 10016

First published in the United States of
America by GALLERY BOOKS
An imprint of W. H. Smith Publishers Inc.
112 Madison Avenue
New York, New York 10016

ISBN 0-8317-6073-7

Printed in the German Democratic
Republic

Acknowledgments
Brian Trodd Publishing House would like
to thank all of the manufacturers,
importers and press agents who have
supplied photographs for this volume.

All photographs from BTPH except:
Laurie Cadell 25, 28; Haymarket
Publications 17.

All artworks supplied by Maltings
Partnership

*This photograph shows a rear view of the
Dodge Daytona.*

Gallery Books Edition ABOVE—

CONTENTS

ALFA ROMEO SPIDER

Alfa Romeo once built many varied sports coupés and convertibles. They now mostly produce more cost-effective saloons to an almost 'Euro-standard' specification, but there is still one 'classic' car carrying that famous laurel-wreathed Milanese emblem: the Alfa Romeo Spider.

Although it has been in production for more than 20 years, the Spider has not aged, which is a testimony to the elegance of Pininfarina's styling. The Spider's engine is a classic all-alloy Alfa twin-cam of 1,962cc which drives through the slick gearbox to the rear wheels. Performance is not exceptional for a sports car with a top speed of 190km/h (118mph), but few cars can match the crisp handling which makes it a delight to drive on twisting roads.

Manufacturer: Alfa Romeo, Italy
Engine: four cylinders; twin ohcs; twin Weber carburettors; 104bhp at 5,500rpm (1,587cc), 128bhp at 5,400rpm (1,962cc)
Gears: five-speed
Capacity: 1,587cc or 1,962cc
Bore and Stroke: 84×88.5mm
Maximum Speed: 190km/h (118mph)
Acceleration: 0–100km/h (0–60mph)=8.9sec
Chassis: rear-wheel drive. Front suspension by wishbones, coil springs, telescopic dampers and anti-roll bar. Rear suspension by coil springs, anti-roll bar and live axle
Dimensions: length 424.18cm (167in); width 163cm (64.2in)
Weight: 1,032.75kg (2,295lb)
Brakes: servo-assisted discs front and rear
Steering: recirculating ball

ASTON MARTIN LAGONDA

Manufacturer: Aston Martin Lagonda, Great Britain
Engine: V8 twin ohcs; four Weber carburettors; 300bhp at 5,000rpm
Gears: three-speed automatic
Capacity: 5,340cc
Bore and Stroke: 100 × 85mm
Maximum Speed: 230km/h (143mph)
Acceleration: 0–100km/h (0–60mph)=7.8sec
Chassis: rear-wheel drive. Aluminium body on a steel chassis. Front suspension by wishbones, coil springs and telescopic dampers. Rear suspension by de Dion, self-levelling
Dimensions: length 528.5cm (208.1in); width 181.6cm (71.5in)
Weight: 2,079kg (4,620lb)
Brakes: dual circuit servo-system with discs front and rear
Steering: power-assisted rack and pinion

When Aston Martin announced the creation of the Lagonda, they saw that there was a market for a four-door luxury sports car saloon, but a succession of problems, mostly with its pioneering digital instrumentation, severely delayed production. By the time these problems were solved, the car's styling began to appear dated.

The Lagonda is based around Aston's classic V8, a four-cam engine which produces enough power to haul the two-ton car to 230km/h (143mph). The car is constructed by craftsmen who hammer the body panels from alumnium sheets and attach them to the steel chassis. It is a skilled operation requiring years of training, and that largely accounts for the Lagonda's high price.

ASTON MARTIN V8 VANTAGE

Manufacturer: Aston Martin Lagonda, Great Britain
Engine: V8 twin ohcs; four Weber carburettors; 360bhp at 6,200rpm
Gears: five-speed
Capacity: 5,340cc
Bore and Stroke: 100 × 85mm
Maximum Speed: 269km/h (168mph)
Acceleration: 0–100km/h (0–60mph)=5.2sec
Chassis: rear-wheel drive. Front suspension by wishbones. Rear suspension by de Dion
Dimensions: length 465cm (183in); width 183cm (72in)
Weight: 1,818kg (4,009lb)
Brakes: discs front and rear
Steering: power-assisted rack and pinion

Ettore Bugatti once labelled the Le Mans Bentleys as 'the fastest lorries in the world', and he would probably attach that damning label to the Aston Martin Vantage were he alive today. The Vantage is immensely fast but it does weigh nearly two tons, which is a lot for a two-door car.

The performance is provided by a 5.3-litre V8 engine which boasts four camshafts and Weber carburettors. Aston Martin rarely quote power figures, but the car undoubtedly needs at least 360bhp from its all-alloy engine for its top speed and superb acceleration. The penalty for such excellent performance is fuel consumption which can dip below 10mpg in extreme conditions. However, that is unlikely to worry the buyer who can afford the Vantage's 'supercar' price tag.

AUDI QUATTRO

The Audi quattro (Audi insist on a small 'q') transformed the world of high-performance motoring when it was announced in 1980, because of its four-wheel drive. Before that time, such systems had only really been used for extra traction off the road, but Audi demonstrated that, even on tarmac, power distributed through four wheels made for better stability and traction, especially in the wet.

The quattro also featured a five-cylinder engine, when four or six-cylinder configurations were the norm, but with the aid of a turbocharger it produced 200bhp and plenty of performance. Others have followed Audi's lead into four-wheel drives, but the quattro remains one of the best high-performance cars on the road.

Manufacturer: Audi, West Germany
Engine: five-cylinder turbocharged fuel-injected; 200bhp at 5,500rpm
Gears: five-speed
Capacity: 2,226cc
Bore and Stroke: 81×86.4mm
Maximum Speed: 222km/h (138mph)
Acceleration: 0–100km/h (0–60mph)=6.2sec
Chassis: four-wheel drive. Front suspension by MacPherson struts. Rear suspension by MacPherson struts and lower wishbones
Dimensions: length 442cm (174in); width 167.6cm (66in)
Weight: 1,053kg (2,340lb)
Brakes: ventilated discs front and rear, with ABS
Steering: power-assisted rack and pinion
Notes: rally version has shorter wheel base. Lockable centre and rear differentials

BERTONE X1/9

When the then Fiat X1/9 was announced in 1972, it was hailed as 'a baby Ferrari': high praise indeed for the little Bertone-styled car built around Fiat 128 running gear. That saloon's front-wheel-drive engine and transmission were put behind the X1/9's cabin to make it mid-engined and endow the machine with the fine handling that this race-style layout offers.

Because of its construction and design, the X1/9 could not be produced as a full convertible, but instead has a lift-off 'Targa'-roof that can be stowed in the front luggage compartment. In 1978, the underpowered 1.3-litre engine became a 1.5, but Fiat found production uneconomic and sold the whole project to Bertone who continue to construct this compact classic themselves.

Manufacturer: Bertone, Italy
Engine: four-cylinder ohc; carburettor
Gears: five-speed
Capacity: 1,498cc
Bore and Stroke: 86.4 × 63.9mm
Maximum Speed: 180km/h (112mph)
Acceleration: 0–100km/h (0–60mph)＝9.5sec
Chassis: mid-engine rear-wheel drive. MacPherson struts front and rear
Dimensions: length 396.2cm (156in); width 157.5cm (62in)
Weight: 913.5kg (2,030lb)
Brakes: discs front and rear
Steering: rack and pinion

From near bankruptcy in the early 1960s, Munich-based BMW have since gone from strength to strength and now mass-manufacture sporting cars of quality which sell well all over the world, and the BMW Z1 comes into this category.

The BMW Z1 is a no-frills roadster which had orders flooding in on the day it was announced.

Based around the company's outstanding 170bhp six-cylinder engine from the 325i, the sleek Z1 has scintillating performance and superb handling and roadholding thanks to its innovative rear suspension. The most novel feature are the doors, which slide down into the sills for easy access, and the car can be driven in this mode too, giving real 'wind-in-the-hair' motoring.

Manufacturer: BMW, West Germany
Engine: six-cylinder; fuel-injected; 170bhp at 5,800rpm
Gears: five-speed manual
Capacity: 2,494cc
Bore and Stroke: 84 × 75mm
Maximum Speed: 225km/h (140mph)
Acceleration: 0–100km/h (0–60mph)=7.9sec
Chassis: rear-wheel drive. Monocoque chassis with plastic body plates. Front suspension by spring struts, rear by Z-axle.
Dimensions: length 392cc (154in); width 169cm (66.5in)
Weight: 1,250kg (2,753lb)
Brakes: discs front and rear with ABS
Steering: power-assisted rack and pinion

CADILLAC ALLANTÉ

Manufacturer: General Motors (Cadillac), USA and Pininfarina, Italy
Engine: V8 ohv; fuel-injected; 200bhp at 4,300rpm
Gears: four-speed automatic
Capacity: 4,087cc
Maximum Speed: 216km/h (135mph)
Acceleration: 0–100km/h (0–60mph)=8.5sec
Chassis: front wheel drive. MacPherson struts front and rear
Dimensions: length 453.6cm (178.6in); width 186.4cm (73.4in)
Weight: 1,570kg (3,490lb)
Brakes: discs front and rear
Notes: Pininfarina designed and manufacture the body in Italy.

The Allanté is Cadillac's attempt to change its old conservative image by competing with the luxury sports coupés and convertibles from Mercedes that many bought in preference to 'Caddys'.

To compete, the car needed some of the same European flair, so the body was designed by Pininfarina (which also clothe Ferraris), and the bodies are even assembled and painted by Pininfarina and airfreighted to the USA for completion. In 1989 General Motors added a more powerful 4.5-litre engine that develops 200bhp for a top speed of 217km/h (135mph). The Allanté is also equipped with the most powerful and elaborate automotive electronics capability in General Motors' history.

CHEVROLET CORVETTE

The 'Vette', as it is affectionately known, has been completely restyled five times since its introduction in 1953, and has had a variety of engines from mild straight-sixes to racing 560bhp V8s. The latest Corvette (the ZR1) is manufactured in glassfibre like its predecessors, and looks equally aggressive. Its V8 engine provides a top speed of 233km/h (145mph), but a Lotus-developed engine has recently become an option, making it a 290km/h (180mph) supercar. The Corvette has LED instrumentation and plastic transverse springs front and rear, but it is mostly a classic 'muscle' car. Nevertheless its handling and roadholding are at least as good as Europe's best sportsters.

Manufacturer: General Motors (Chevrolet), USA
Engine: V8 ohv; fuel-injected; 245bhp at 4,000rpm
Gears: four-speed manual or four-speed automatic
Capacity: 5,735cc
Bore and Stroke: 101.6 × 88.4mm
Maximum Speed: 233km/h (145mph)
Acceleration: 0–100km/h (0–60mph)=6sec
Chassis: rear-wheel drive. Front suspension by wishbones and leaf spring. Rear suspension by multilinks and leaf spring
Dimensions: length 448.56cm (176.6in); width 180.5cm (71.1in)
Weight: 1,449kg (3,220lb)
Brakes: discs front and rear
Steering: power-assisted rack and pinion

CHRYSLER MASERATI

Manufacturer: Chrysler, USA
Engine: four-cylinder ohc fuel-injected turbo; 174bhp at 5,200rpm, or 16-valve dual ohc; 208bhp at 5,500rpm
Gears: five-speed manual or three-speed automatic
Capacity: 2,213cc
Bore and Stroke: 87.5 × 92mm
Maximum Speed: 209.3–217.4km/h (130–135mph)
Chassis: front-wheel drive. Front suspension by MacPherson struts. Rear suspension by dead axle
Dimensions: length 446.53cm (175.8in); width 173.99cm (68.5in)
Weight: 1,363.5kg (3,030lb)
Brakes: ventilated discs front and rear

The Chrysler Maserati's story is similar to the Cadillac Allanté's in being an attempt to give an American car Italian flair. Maserati are renowned for engines, but curiously their contribution to the convertible was the body and trim. Chrysler considered that their own undoubtedly excellent 2.2-litre overhead-cam four was the perfect engine for the project, and when turbocharged it gave 174bhp. The car was even better when given the Lotus-designed 16-valve twin-cam head in 1988.

Both engines were allied to a five-speed manual transmission and, with disc brakes all around, this American-Italian hybrid has lived up to its famous Italian badge and the outstanding cars that have previously worn that badge.

Industrialist Alejandro De Tomaso virtually bought the whole of the Italian motor-bike industry in the 1960s, and then decided to build a supercar bearing his own name, with a badge based on his native Argentinian flag. However, instead of building his own engines as his Modenese neighbours Lamborghini and Ferrari had done, he used a convenient Ford V8 in his supercar which he named *Pantera* (Panther). Many enthusiasts felt that the inclusion of an American engine, however good, somehow detracted from the car's Italian charisma, and sales were initially disappointing.

The top-of-the-range GT5-S Pantera has a top speed of 266km/h (165mph) as well as fierce acceleration, and is held to the road by the widest tyres Pirelli make.

Manufacturer: De Tomaso, Italy
Engine: V8 ohv; carburettor; 350bhp at 5,600rpm
Gears: five-speed
Capacity: 5,763cc
Bore and Stroke: 101.6 × 88.9mm
Maximum Speed: 265km/h (165mph)
Acceleration: 0–100km/h (0–60mph) = 5.8sec
Chassis: mid-engine rear-wheel drive. Suspension by wishbones front and rear
Dimensions: length 426.97cm (168.1in); width 182.88cm (72in)
Weight: 1,408.5kg (3,130lb)
Brakes: dual circuit, discs front and rear

DODGE DAYTONA

Dodge is the division of Chrysler responsible for performance cars, and can take credit for the Daytona. This is an excellent example of how a very good sports coupé can be developed from a humble saloon, in this case it was the Dodge Aries/Plymouth Reliant which was the starting point for the Chrysler 'K-car'.

The K-car was a well-balanced saloon with front-wheel drive, and from it Chrysler developed a range of models including the Daytona. From the early days with just the ordinary 2.2-litre ohc four (virtually Chrysler's only engine), it has developed with turbo-charging and intercooling to produce 174bhp. The Daytona is a good example of how the USA has adapted to produce good, small sports cars.

Manufacturer: Chrysler (Dodge), USA
Engine: four-cylinder ohc; fuel-injected; 100bhp at 4800rpm (2,501cc), 146bhp at 5,200rpm (2,213cc) and 174bhp at 5,200rpm (turbo-intercooler)
Gears: five-speed manual and three-speed automatic
Capacity: 2,501cc, 2,213cc and turbo
Bore and Stroke: 87.5 × 92mm
Maximum Speed: 217.4km/h (135mph)
Chassis: front-wheel drive. Front suspension by MacPherson struts. Rear suspension by dead axle
Dimensions: length 444.5cm (175in); width 176cm (69.3in)
Weight: 1,206–1,291.5kg (2,680–2,870lb)
Brakes: discs front and rear

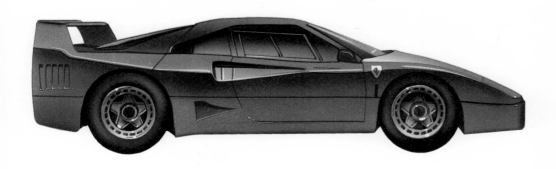

The name simply refers to the model which Ferrari built to commemorate their fortieth anniversary. It is probably the most thinly disguised racing car that has ever been offered for road use; indeed, two decades ago, an unmodified F40 could probably have won Le Mans.

Some consider the interior to be too spartan, but this is compensated for by the car's speed. The heart of the F40 is a twin turbo V8 engine that is loosely based on the 328 motor, but the F40 can generate 478bhp to give a top speed of 322km/h (200mph) with lightning acceleration. Grand Prix driver Gerhard Berger believes that only a few racing drivers could exploit fully the F40's abilities, such are its strengths in roadholding, acceleration and braking.

Manufacturer: Ferrari, Italy
Engine: V8 dual ohc; 32-valve twin turbo; fuel-injected; 478bhp at 7,000rpm
Gears: five-speed manual
Capacity: 2,936cc
Bore and Stroke: 82×69.5mm
Maximum Speed: 323.8km/h (201.3mph)
Acceleration: 0–100km/h (0–60mph)=3.8sec
Chassis: mid-engine rear-wheel drive. Suspension by wishbones front and rear
Dimensions: length 442.97cm (174.4in); width 198.12cm (78in)
Weight: 1,091.25kg (2,425lb)
Brakes: discs front and rear
Steering: rack and pinion

FERRARI 208 TURBO

Italy has a punitive luxury-car tax for all vehicles over 2,000cc, and only the very rich can afford cars that are any larger. However, a turbocharger can improve performance in a way which only an increase in engine capacity can otherwise achieve. Therefore, the Ferrari 208 (20 for 2.0 litres: 8 for 8 cylinders) has the same performance as the 328 Quattrovalvole, costs more before tax, but costs *less* once tax has been added. Of course, it is sold only in Italy.

The car is slower than the Ferrari 308, and its fuel consumption is much worse. Everything else is comparable though, and its handling and roadholding are of the highest order, but few are produced.

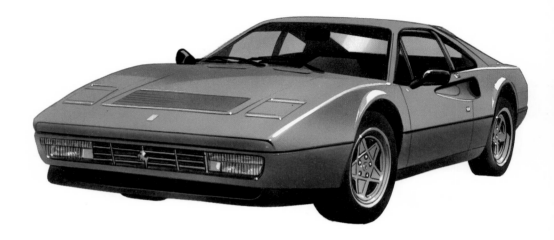

Manufacturer: Ferrari, Italy
Engine: V8 dual ohc; fuel-injected; turbocharged; 220bhp at 6,500rpm
Gears: five-speed manual
Capacity: 1,991cc
Bore and Stroke: 82×69.5mm
Maximum Speed: 241km/h (150mph)
Acceleration: 0–100km/h (0–60mph)=5.2sec
Chassis: mid-engine rear-wheel drive. Suspension by wishbones front and rear
Dimensions: length 425.25cm (167.5in); width 172.72cm (68in)
Weight: 1,255.5kg (2,790lb)
Brakes: discs front and rear
Steering: rack and pinion
Notes: this model may be found only in Italy.

FERRARI TESTAROSSA

Manufacturer: Ferrari, Italy
Engine: flat 12 48-valve; fuel-injected; 390bhp at 6,300rpm
Gears: five-speed manual
Capacity: 4,942cc
Bore and Stroke: 82 × 78mm
Maximum Speed: 298.8km/h (180mph)
Acceleration: 0–100km/h (0–60mph)=5.8sec
Chassis: mid-engine rear-wheel drive. Suspension by wishbones front and rear
Dimensions: length 448.56cm (176.6in); width 197.6cm (77.8in)
Weight: 1,494kg (3,320lb)
Brakes: ventilated discs front and rear
Steering: rack and pinion

The original 1950s Testa Rossa (it was then two words meaning 'red head') was so named because its engine's cylinder head was painted that colour. The latest Testarossa does still have red cylinder heads but, unlike most other road-going Ferraris, its 12 cylinders are not set in a vee but horizontally oppose each other. The pistons of each bank of six move towards each other as the crankshaft turns, rather like fists punching. There are 48 valves in its 5-litre engine, which produce 390bhp which gives the car a maximum speed of 298.8km/h (180mph).

Although low and sleek, this Pininfarina-styled car is wider than a Rolls-Royce and this plus its 1.5-ton weight hamper it on tight corners. On open highways though, the Testarossa leaves the opposition standing.

FORD MUSTANG

Manufacturer: Ford, USA
Engine: 4-cylinder ohc; fuel-injected; 90bhp at 4,200rpm; V8 ohv: 225bhp at 4,200rpm
Gears: 5-speed manual; 4-speed automatic
Capacity: 2,301cc or 4,942cc (V8)
Bore and Stroke: 96 × 79.4mm
Maximum Speed: 159.4–209.3km/h (99–130mph)
Acceleration: 0–100km/h (0–60mph)=11.2sec (2.3lit) or 7sec (5lit)
Chassis: rear-wheel drive. Front suspension by wishbones. Rear suspension by live axle
Dimensions: length 456.18cm (179.6in); width 175.5cm (69.1in)
Weight: 1,238–1,328.9kg (2,751–2,953lb)
Brakes: front discs, rear drums
Steering: power-assisted rack and pinion

The classic front-engine, rear-drive Mustang should be coming to the end of its life now, ending a line that began back in 1964, yet popular demand keeps it going. That is unsurprising. The current car may not have the incredible appeal of the first one, which sold in record numbers on its first day, nor the sheer horsepower of those in the late 1960s, but the current GT is no mean performer. Its 5-litre V8 engine pumps out 225bhp to give wonderful acceleration of 7 seconds to 100km/h (60mph).

With a live rear axle and a basically old chassis design, the Mustang is an unsophisticated performer, particularly when compared with the modern Corvette; but it is honest, rugged and fast.

HONDA PRELUDE

Manufacturer: Honda, Japan
Engine: four-cylinder ohc; carburettor; 106bhp at 5,500rpm, or dual ohc 16-valve fuel-injected; 137bhp at 6,000rpm
Gears: five-speed manual or four-speed automatic
Capacity: 1,830cc or 1,958cc (dohc)
Bore and Stroke: 80 × 91mm
Maximum Speed: 176km/h (109.4mph); 201km/h (125mph) (dual ohc)
Acceleration: 0–100km/h (0–60mph)=10.5sec (1.8) or 8.3sec (2.0lit)
Chassis: front wheel drive. Front suspension by wishbones. Rear suspension by MacPherson struts
Dimensions: length 429.5cm (169.1in); width 168.9cm (66.5in)
Weight: 947.25–1,021.5kg (2,105–2,270lb)
Brakes: discs front and rear with ABS
Steering: power-assisted four-wheel steering

When a car goes round a corner, each wheel helps to steer it. Because of this reasoned Honda, all four wheels ought to be actively steered and so they introduced such a system on their Honda Prelude sports coupé. This is a quick machine, and the extra crispness of the four-wheel-steer handling makes it stand out from the opposition.

As the Prelude's steering is turned slightly, so the rear wheels steer in the same direction as the front wheels, but at a shallower angle to give extra stability. When the wheel is turned more, as when negotiating a tight corner, the rear wheels steer in the opposite direction and the car 'crabs' easily around. It takes time to become accustomed to the Prelude's steering, but the complexities are justified by the extra agility such a system offers.

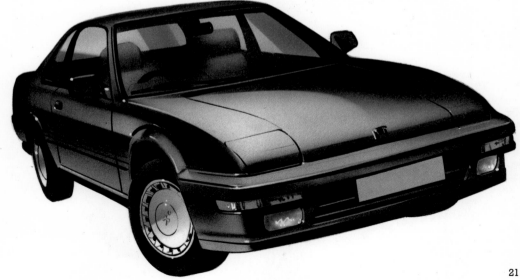

ISUZU PIAZZA

Manufacturer: Isuzu, Japan
Engine: four-cylinder ohc; fuel-injected; 102bhp at 5,400rpm, or dual ohc 116bhp at 6,200rpm, or turbo 152bhp at 5,400rpm
Gears: five-speed manual or three-speed automatic
Capacity: 1,950cc or 1,995cc (turbo)
Bore and Stroke: 88 × 82mm
Maximum Speed: 170.66–209.3km/h (106–130mph)
Acceleration: 0–100km/h (0–60mph)=8.4sec
Chassis: rear-wheel drive. Front suspension by wishbones. Rear suspension by live axle
Dimensions: length 438.4cm (172.6in); width 165.6cm (65.2in)
Weight: 1,131.75–1,181.25kg (2,515–2,625lb)
Brakes: discs front and rear

The latest Isuzu Piazza Turbo is a three-way marriage between Japan, Italy and Great Britain. The Japanese manufacturer went to Ital Design in Italy who had the 'Piazza' already designed as a concept car which they hoped would be the second-generation Volkswagen Scirocco. Then, after early criticism of their machine's handling and roadholding, Isuzu asked Lotus to develop their car's chassis.

Although the Piazza is a little old-fashioned in design with its live rear axle, it now handles very well indeed. It is not short of power either, because 152bhp is available from its turbocharged 2-litre engine.

The XJS may not be the prettiest car ever to leave Jaguar's factory, but the big sports coupé has certainly sold very well, especially in America.

Although it was first used in the E-Type, Jaguar's superb V12 engine was really intended for their XJ saloon and XJS coupé. When the latter finally appeared, it boasted a top speed of almost 241km/h (150mph) and a smoothness and refinement which made even Rolls-Royces seem a little coarse.

The XJS was offered first as a Cabriolet with lift-off roof panels and a fold-down rear hood, and then as a full convertible. Meanwhile, Jaguar's new 24-valve AJ6 3.6-litre six-cylinder engine was offered in the XJS, although it was primarily intended for Jaguar's new range of saloons.

Manufacturer: Jaguar, Great Britain
Engine: six-cylinder; 24-valve dual ohc; fuel-injected; 225bhp at 5,300rpm, or V12 ohc; 295bhp at 5,500rpm
Gears: five-speed manual, four-speed and three-speed automatic
Capacity: 3,590cc (6 cyl), 5,345cc (V12)
Bore and Stroke: 91 × 92mm (6 cyl), 90 × 70mm (V12)
Maximum Speed: 220.1km/h (136.8mph); 235km/h (146mph) (V12)
Acceleration: 0–100km/h (0–60mph)=7.6sec (XJS 3.6), or 7.9sec (V12)
Chassis: rear-wheel drive. Suspension by wishbones front and rear
Dimensions: length 476.5cm (187.6in); width 179.3cm (70.6in)
Weight: 1,647–1,741.5kg (3,660–3,870lb)
Brakes: discs front and rear
Steering: rack and pinion

LAMBORGHINI COUNTACH

Manufacturer: Lamborghini, Italy
Engine: V12 48-valve; dual ohc;
carburettor; 455bhp at 7,000rpm
Gears: five-speed
Capacity: 5,167cc
Bore and Stroke: 85.5 × 75mm
Maximum Speed: 294.6km/h (183mph)
Acceleration: 0–100km/h
(0–60mph)=4.8sec
Chassis: mid-engine rear-wheel drive.
Suspension by wishbones front and rear
Dimensions: length 420.1cm (165.4in);
width 199.9cm (78.7cm)
Weight: 1,478.25kg (3,285lb)
Brakes: ventilated discs front and rear
Steering: rack and pinion

The Lamborghini Countach is undoubtedly the most 'super' supercar. Lamborghini certainly made an impact with the Miura, but it was the Bertone-styled Countach of 1971 which set the seal on their credibility and profitability.

The latest and last Countach is powered by a 5.2-litre 48-valve V12 engine mounted behind the driver. The engine's 455bhp give the Countach a rocket-like acceleration, and the car reaches a speed of more than 290km/h (180mph). That is coupled to a chassis which allows the big automobile to corner more quickly that even Grand Prix machines could manage two decades ago, and its flip-top doors almost make it practical around town!

Manufacturer: Lamborghini, Italy
Engine: V8 dual ohc; carburettors; 255bhp at 7,000rpm
Gears: five-speed
Capacity: 3,485cc
Bore and Stroke: 86 × 75mm
Maximum Speed: 247.9km/h (154mph)
Acceleration: 0–100km/h (0–60mph)=5.8sec
Chassis: mid-engine rear-wheel drive. Suspension by MacPherson struts front and rear
Dimensions: length 433cm (170.5in); width 187.9cm (74in)
Weight: 1,487.25kg (3,305lb)
Brakes: ventilated discs front and rear
Steering: rack and pinion

Lamborghini, as well as competing against the Ferrari Boxer with its Countach, decided to attack the market held by its rival's 308 and 328 models. Hence, Lamborghini have had their runs of 'junior supercars' with the Silhouette and Urraco. The latest in this line is the Jalpa, a Bertone-styled 'Targa'-type car powered by the latest in Lamborghini's range of V8 engines. This particular engine is of 3.5 litres and produces 255bhp. Despite being a 'junior' supercar, it is still a big vehicle, tipping the scales at almost 1.5 tons, which means it is heavier than the Countach.

Although it has simple MacPherson strut suspension all round, its handling is unmatched at any price.

LOTUS ESPRIT

Lotus were once renowned for their small sports cars, but the company's policy for car production changed in the early 1970s, and a move upmarket was planned to compete with Porsche and even Ferrari. The front-engined Elite was soon followed by a new mid-engined car: the Esprit. Styled by the Ital Design company, the Esprit looked good and certainly held the road as well as its illustrious predecessors. Unfortunately, it simply did not have enough power.

That was remedied when the Turbo Esprit was announced, and that plus a subtle yet attractive styling update in 1988 has made the Esprit a success. Lotus have now proved that they can compete favourably with the opposition . . . and this has been achieved at a fraction of the price.

Manufacturer: Lotus, Great Britain
Engine: four-cylinder 16-valve dual ohc; Dellorto carburettors; 172bhp at 6,500rpm (2.2lit), or turbo 215bhp at 6,000rpm
Gears: five-speed manual
Capacity: 2,174cc
Bore and Stroke: 95.3 × 76.2mm
Maximum Speed: 223.8km/h (139mph) (2.2lit); 244.7km/h (152mph) (turbo)
Acceleration: 0–100km/h (0–60mph)=5.4sec
Chassis: mid-engine rear-wheel drive; wishbone suspension front and trailing radius arms rear
Dimensions: length 419.1cm (165in); width 185.4cm (73in)
Weight: 1,020kg (2,248lb)
Brakes: discs front and rear
Steering: rack and pinion

Manufacturer: Lotus, Great Britain
Engine: four-cylinder 16-valve dual ohc; carburettors; 162bhp at 6,500rpm
Gears: five-speed manual or four-speed automatic
Capacity: 2,174cc
Bore and Stroke: 95.3 × 76.2mm
Maximum Speed: 215.74km/h (134mph)
Acceleration: 0–100km/h (0–60mph)=7.2sec
Chassis: rear-wheel drive. Composite body on steel chassis. Suspension by wishbones front and trailing radius arms rear
Dimensions: length 437.38cm (172.2in); width 181.61cm (71.5in)
Weight: 1,125kg (2,500lb)
Brakes: discs front and rear
Steering: rack and pinion

The Excel developed from the Eclat, itself a derivative of the Elite, and takes the Norfolk company into the 1990s with a competitive sports 2+2. Like all Lotuses, the Excel has a steel backbone chassis to which is attached its glassfibre body. Lotus have been using this material in their cars for more than 30 years, and their expertise with it is second to none.

Like the Esprit, the Excel uses a 16-valve, four-cylinder engine which is canted over to allow the car a more aerodynamically efficient nose. An SE version of the Excel has an engine in a higher state of tuning, and has a top speed of almost 224km/h (140mph), while the SA is an automatic version.

MASERATI BITURBO

Manufacturer: Maserati, Italy
Engine: V6 dual ohc twin turbo; fuel-injected; 200bhp at 5,500rpm
Gears: Five-speed manual or three-speed automatic
Capacity: 2,491cc
Bore and Stroke: 91.6 × 63mm
Maximum Speed: 225.4km/h (140mph)
Acceleration: 0–100km/h (0–60mph)=6.6sec (2 door and convertible) or 6.3sec (4 door)
Chassis: rear-wheel drive. Two and four door versions. Front suspension by MacPherson struts. Rear suspension by semi-trailing arms
Dimensions: length 439.9cm (173.2in); width 172.9cm (68.1in)
Weight: 1,264.5kg (2,810lb)
Brakes: discs front and rear
Steering: power-assisted rack and pinion
Notes: convertible is called a Spyder

Maserati's sole major rivals were once Ferrari, but the company was badly hit by the arrival of yet another illustrious neighbour, Lamborghini. Maserati's production declined, and the future looked bleak. Part-owner Alejandro de Tomaso decided that, instead of building limited-edition super-cars, they would move the models slightly downmarket by initiating a new range of cars called 'Biturbo' (named after the standard V6 engine's twin superchargers).

Unusually, the V6 engine has three valves per cylinder (two inlet and one exhaust) rather than the more usual two or four, but later versions are promised with even more valves.

In 2.5-litre form, the injected engine produces 200bhp.

Manufacturer: Mazda, Japan
Engine: Wankel rotary engine; fuel-injected; 150bhp at 6,500rpm
Gears: five-speed manual or three-speed automatic
Capacity: 2,616cc equivalent
Maximum Speed: 215.74km/h (134mph)
Acceleration: 0–100km/h (0–60mph)=8.6sec
Chassis: rear-wheel drive. Front suspension by MacPherson struts. Rear suspension by multilinks
Dimensions: length 429cm (168.9in); width 168.9cm (66.5in)
Weight: 1,194.75–1,300.5kg (2,655–2,890lb)
Brakes: discs front and rear
Steering: recirculating ball
Notes: only production car with a rotary engine

In the 1960s, the Wankel rotary engine was looked on as a breakthrough in engine design. It proved unreliable, however, and today only the Japanese Mazda company persists with the design. This is a shame, because a Wankel is much more compact than a conventional engine, is also lighter, and produces prodigious amounts of power.

The twin-rotor motor in the Mazda RX7 is almost lost in the car's engine bay, and its smallness allows it to be set well back in the chassis for better weight distribution. The major drawback to the Wankel is its thirst for fuel, especially as conventional multivalve engines have become so efficient in recent years. Nevertheless, the RX7 has a worldwide cult following.

MERCEDES BENZ SL

Luxury, prestige, status and speed – the Mercedes sports coupés and convertibles have them all in an enviable formula that has not needed to be changed for years.

Under the skin, which was last revised in 1986, is the traditional front-engine and rear-drive layout with engines ranging from a 2.9-litre straight-six through to the alloy overhead-cam 5-litre V8 engine which gives 245bhp to the top of the range 500SL. There is no manual gearbox option but a fine, four-speed automatic transmission. Mercedes' customers expect comfort rather than a 'true' sports car ride, and the SL wishbone front and semi-trailing-arm rear suspension helps provide it while still giving perfect control.

Manufacturer: Daimler-Benz, West Germany
Engine: straight-six ohc; fuel-injected; 188bhp at 5,700rpm; or V8 ohc (4.2lit), 218bhp at 5,150rpm; or V8 ohc (5lit), 245bhp at 4,750rpm
Gears: four-speed automatic
Capacity: 2,962cc (straight-six), 4,196cc (V8) or 4,973cc (V8)
Bore and Stroke: 88.5 × 88.25mm
Maximum Speed: 198–215.7km/h (123–134mph)
Acceleration: 0–100km/h (0–60mph) = 9.1sec
Chassis: rear-wheel drive. Front suspension by wishbones. Rear-suspension by semi-trailing arms.
Dimensions: length 439.9cm (173in); width 177.8cm (70in)
Weight: 1,511–1,608kg (3,326–3,539lb)
Brakes: discs front and rear with ABS
Steering: recirculating ball

MITSUBISHI STARION

Manufacturer: Mitsubishi, Japan
Engine: four-cylinder ohc; fuel-injected turbo (2 litre); 180bhp at 3,500rpm, or 12-valve 200bhp at 6,000rpm, or fuel-injected (2.6 litre); 155bhp at 5,000rpm
Gears: five-speed manual or three-speed automatic
Capacity: 1,997cc or 2,555cc
Bore and Stroke: 84×90mm or 91.1×98mm
Maximum Speed: 210.9–220.5km/h (131–137mph)
Acceleration: 0–100km/h (0–60mph)=6.5sec (turbo)
Chassis: rear-wheel drive. Suspension by MacPherson struts front and rear
Dimensions: length 439.9cm (173.2in); width 168.4cm (66.3in)
Weight: 1,219.5–1,269kg (2,710–2,820lb)
Brakes: ventilated discs front and rear
Steering: power-assisted recirculating ball

The Mitsubishi Starion in its wide-bodied Turbo form has more character than any other Japanese sports car. And, as with other characterful designs, that is probably as much by accident as design.

Its looks are uncompromising and aggressive (the extended-arch wide look is reminiscent of the Porsche 944), and they perfectly mirror the feel of the car. It is a traditional, front-engine, rear-drive design using MacPherson struts all round. Handling characteristics are quite distinct, because Mitsubishi had the courage to build a car for the enthusiast in that it oversteers at will with a sharp response to the steering.

No one could pretend that the Starion is sophisticated in any respect, but that is part of its great charm.

PANTHER SOLO

It was a great surprise when the company announced the Solo, which was to be nothing less than a turbocharged, four-wheel-drive sports car for the mass market. The project has been delayed at various times, but the passage of time has not made the car any less impressive.

Power from the Solo comes from the now legendary Sierra Cosworth engine: this is a 16-valve four-cylinder engine with a turbocharger which produces 204bhp in standard form, and is mid-mounted in the Solo.

The Ferguson-developed four-wheel-drive system ensures that the Solo corners well, and anti-lock braking completes this attractive package.

Manufacturer: Panther, Great Britain
Engine: four-cylinder 16 valve dual ohc; fuel-injected turbo; 204bhp at 6,000rpm
Gears: five-speed manual
Capacity: 1,993cc
Bore and Stroke: 90.82 × 76.95mm
Maximum Speed: 241.5km/h (150mph)
Acceleration: 0–100km/h (0–60mph)=5.7sec
Chassis: mid-engine four-wheel drive through a Ferguson transmission. Body made from advanced composite materials mounted on a steel chassis. Front suspension by MacPherson struts. Rear suspension by wishbones
Dimensions: length 434.34cm (171in); width 178cm (70.1in)
Weight: 1,089kg (2,420lb)
Brakes: discs on front and rear use ABS.
Steering: rack and pinion
Notes: uses Ford Sierra Cosworth engine

Manufacturer: Pontiac, USA
Engine: four-cylinder ohv; fuel-injected; 98bhp at 4,800rpm, or V6 ohv; 135bhp at 4,500rpm
Gears: five-speed manual or three-speed automatic
Capacity: 2,471cc or 2,838cc (V6)
Maximum Speed: 185.15–193.2km/h (115–120mph)
Chassis: mid-engine rear-wheel drive. Moulded plastic composite body attached to a metal skeleton. Front suspension by wishbones. Rear suspension by MacPherson struts
Dimensions: length 414.27–419.35cm (163.1–165.1in); width 175cm (68.9in)
Weight: 1,170–1,255.5kg (2,600–2,790lb)
Brakes: discs front and rear
Steering: rack and pinion

America's only mid-engined sports car is one of the most interesting models ever built by General Motors. It used suspension parts from Pontiac's version of the Chevette and an old pushrod four-cylinder engine, yet these ordinary parts were assembled into a chassis unlike any other. Called a 'spaceframe', it was really a steel monocoque on which were hung the plastic body panels. This system allows very easy restyling, and indeed the Fiero has changed shape considerably since its introduction in 1983. The first cars were not especially fast, but the introduction of the larger, 2.8-litre V6 engine increased the Fiero's performance dramatically, although it lacks the precise feel of some mid-engined rivals.

PONTIAC FIREBIRD

Manufacturer: General Motors (Pontiac), USA
Engine: V6 ohv; fuel-injected; 135bhp at 3,900rpm, or V8 (5lit); 215bhp at 4,400rpm, or V8 (5.7lit); 225bhp at 4,400rpm
Gears: five-speed manual or four-speed automatic
Capacity: 2,838cc (V6), 5,001cc (V8) or 5,733cc (V8)
Maximum Speed: 169–209.3km/h (105–130mph)
Acceleration: 0–100km/h (0–60mph)=6.9sec
Chassis: rear-wheel drive. Front suspension by MacPherson struts. Rear suspension by live axle
Dimensions: length 477.77–486.66cm (188.1–191.6in); width 183.89cm (72.4in)
Weight: 1,392.75–1,532.25kg (3,095–3,405lb)
Brakes: front discs and rear drums
Steering: recirculating ball

The Pontiac Firebird, with its almost identical (under the skin) sister the Chevrolet Camaro, was General Motors' answer to the Ford Mustang in being a simple and affordable sports car. There have been various Firebirds since 1967: the current model is very nimble for a traditional rear-wheel-drive design. The early Firebird was called America's best handling car, and the present version carries on that tradition and, remarkably, does it by using a coilsprung live axle as well as recirculating-ball steering.

The top of the range model, the Trans-Am, shares the Corvette's 5.7-litre V8 in 225bhp trim which gives an acceleration that allows the Pontiac to break the 7 second 0–100km/h (0–60mph) barrier.

Manufacturer: Porsche, West Germany
Engine: flat-6 ohc; fuel-injected; 231bhp at 5,900rpm, or turbo; 300bhp at 5,500rpm
Gears: five-speed manual
Capacity: 3,164cc or 3,299cc (Turbo)
Bore and Stroke: 95 × 74.4mm (Carrera); 97 × 74.4mm (Turbo)
Maximum Speed: 244.72–275.31km/h (152–171mph)
Acceleration: 0–100km/h (0–60mph)=5.9sec (911 Carrera), 5.2sec (Turbo)
Chassis: rear-engine rear-wheel drive. Front suspension by MacPherson struts and torsion bars. Rear suspension semi-trailing arms and torsion bars
Dimensions: length 429cm (168.9in); width 165.1–177.5cm (65–69.9in)
Weight: 1,201.5–1,325.25kg (2,670–2,945lb)
Brakes: discs front and rear
Steering: rack and pinion

Porsche wanted to stop producing their rear-engined sports cars and concentrate on their new breed of front-engined cars, but demand has never wavered for the 911 series, and Porsche have had to keep producing them. The 911 was first seen in 1963: since then there have been hardly any changes in styling on the car, which looks as fresh as ever.

The top of the range is the 911 Turbo (actually designated the Type 930). The car's 3.3-litre boosted engine generates 300bhp for a top speed of 275km/h (171mph) and excellent acceleration. Its rear-mounted engine means that much of its weight is at the back, and this makes handling in extreme conditions tricky; this is arguably the car's main weakness.

PORSCHE 928S4

When the 928 appeared in 1977, it was a complete contrast to the 911 that it was intended to replace (but never did). The engine was a water-cooled V8 rather than an air-cooled flat six, and was mounted in the front rather than the back. From its origins as a mild, if powerful, Grand Tourer, the 928 developed steadily and became ever faster. Yet despite its spectacular performance, the 928 is the most untemperamental of cars to drive: this is a testament to its chassis, which has the transmission mounted at the rear for perfect weight distribution, as well as to Porsche's unique rear-suspension design (the 'Weissach' axle) which gives precise rear-wheel control in all conditions.

Manufacturer: Porsche, West Germany
Engine: V8 32-valve dual ohc; fuel-injected; 320bhp at 6,000rpm
Gears: five-speed manual or four-speed automatic
Capacity: 4,957cc
Bore and Stroke: 97×78.9mm
Maximum Speed: 268.87km/h (167mph)
Acceleration: 0–100km/h (0–60mph)=5.9sec
Chassis: rear-wheel drive with rear-mounted gearbox. Front suspension by MacPherson struts. Rear suspension by multilinks
Dimensions: length 452.12cm (178in); width 183.38cm (72.2in)
Weight: 1,568.25kg (3,485lb)
Brakes: ventilated discs front and rear with ABS
Steering: power-assisted rack and pinion

Manufacturer: Porsche, West Germany
Engine: four-cylinder; fuel-injected 165bhp at 5,800rpm
Gears: five-speed manual or three-speed automatic
Capacity: 2,681cc
Bore and Stroke: 104 × 78.9mm
Maximum Speed: 220km/h (137mph)
Acceleration: 0–100km/h (0–60mph)=8.2sec
Chassis: rear-wheel drive with rear-mounted gearbox. Front suspension by MacPherson struts. Rear suspension by semi-trailing arms and torsion bars
Dimensions: length 419.86cm (165.3in); width 173.48cm (68.3in)
Weight: 1,290kg (2,844lb)
Brakes: ventilated discs front and rear
Steering: power-assisted rack and pinion

Many enthusiasts detested the first of Porsche's new breed of front-engined cars: the 924 from which grew the 944. Not only was it a discarded Audi project, but its engine was derived from a Volkswagen Caravanette! Since then Porsche have steadily developed these models, and the latest Series 2 cars are true Porsches and are priced accordingly.

The 944 is now the base model and has a 2.7-litre four-cylinder engine canted over at the front. Power is taken to the gearbox, which is united with the rear axle for more even weight distribution. There is also a 16-valve version of the 944 which is noticeably faster. Finally, the top-of-the-range 944 Turbo, with its 3-litre engine, has real supercar performance.

PORSCHE 959

Manufacturer: Porsche, West Germany
Engine: flat-6 24-valve dual ohc; fuel-injected turbo; 450bhp at 6,500rpm
Gears: six-speed manual
Capacity: 2,850cc
Bore and Stroke: 95 × 67mm
Maximum Speed: 315.56km/h (196mph)
Acceleration: 0–100km/h
(0–60mph)=3.9sec
Chassis: rear-engine four-wheel drive.
Suspension by wishbones front and rear
Dimensions: length 425.95cm (167.7in);
width 183.89cm (72.4in)
Weight: 1,440kg (3,220lb)
Brakes: discs front and rear
Steering: power-assisted rack and pinion

The Porsche 959 is a *tour de force*, the Stuttgart company showing that they could take their traditional rear-engined layout and develop from it a car that would have few if any peers.

The 959's engine is developed from the 911 flat-six range, but in this form it has water-cooled cylinder heads rather than full air-cooling as have the 911s. It is also equipped with twin turbochargers and no less than 450bhp from its 2,850cc. The greatest innovation of the 959 is its computer-controlled four-wheel drive which ensures perfect balance under all conditions. Coming out of a corner, for instance, the computer allocates more power to the rear wheels for better traction. Should the system feel those wheels start to spin, however, it instantaneously allocates more power to the front to pull the 959 out of trouble. Only the Ferrari F40 can match the Porsche 959's acceleration, but the Porsche's acceleration hardly varies even if it is dry, wet or snowing.

Manufacturer: Reliant, Great Britain
Engine: four-cylinder ohc; carburettor; 72bhp at 5,600rpm (1.4lit), or 95bhp at 5,600rpm (1.6lit), or fuel-injected turbo (1.8lit) 135bhp at 6,000rpm
Gears: four or five-speed manual
Capacity: 1,393cc, 1,598cc or 1,809cc (turbo)
Bore and Stroke: 80×64.5mm, 80×79.5mm or 93×68.5mm
Maximum Speed: 159.39–204.47km/h (99–127mph)
Acceleration: 0–100km/h (0–60mph)=12.7sec (1.4), 9.6sec (1.6), 7.6sec (1.8i)
Chassis: rear-wheel drive. Plastic composite body. Front suspension by wishbones. Rear suspension by semi-trailing arms
Dimensions: length 388.36cm (152.9in); width 157.98cm (62.2in)
Weight: 832.5–882kg (1,850–1,960lb)
Brakes: front discs and rear drums
Steering: rack and pinion
Notes: uses Ford 1.4 and 1.6 engines and Nissan 1.8i engine

Reliant went to the Italian designer Michelotti for the plastic-composite body of their first proper sports car. He had, after all designed the Triumph Spitfire and the TR4 among others, but unfortunately his idiosyncratic design hid the car's many good qualities. It made the little Reliant seem like a toy rather than a serious sports car.

The SS1's outstanding chassis gave excellent handling and roadholding far surpassing that of any traditional British sports car. Power came from Ford's XR3 engine, but this was insufficient and it was later replaced by the Nissan 1.8-litre ohc, fuel-injected turbo engine. Finally, the car appeared at the 1988 Birmingham Motor Show in the attractive body it should have had initially, designed by William Towns.

RENAULT GTA

This attractive sports car is known as the Alpine in Europe and as the GTA in Great Britain where another manufacturer holds the copyright on that name. In fact, the car is manufactured in Dieppe, France by Alpine, which is a subsidiary of Renault.

This car follows all its predecessors (of which the most famous was the A110, which dominated international rallying for many years) and the Porsche 911 in that its engine is rear-mounted. This engine, the V6, is either a normally aspirated 2.8 litres or a turbocharged 2.5 litres. The car's body is made of many high-tech materials, and its style makes it probably the most futuristic-looking production car on sale.

Manufacturer: Renault, France
Engine: V6 ohc; fuel-injected; 160bhp at 5,700rpm, or turbo 200bhp at 5,750rpm. Uses Garrett turbocharger
Gears: five-speed manual
Capacity: 2,849cc or 2,458cc (turbo)
Bore and Stroke: 91 × 73mm or 91 × 63mm (turbo)
Maximum Speed: 235–249.55km/h (146–155mph)
Acceleration: 0–100km/h (0–60mph)=7.7sec (2.8), 6.0sec (2.5 turbo)
Chassis: rear-engine rear-wheel drive. Composite body bonded onto a steel backbone chassis. Suspension by wishbones front and rear plus coil springs and anti-roll bars
Dimensions: length 433cm (170.5in); width 110.9cm (68.9in)
Weight: 1,100–1,201.5kg (2,445–2,670lb)
Brakes: ventilated discs front and rear
Steering: rack and pinion

Manufacturer: Subaru, Japan
Engine: flat-four ohc; fuel-injected turbo; 136bhp at 3,600rpm
Gears: five-speed manual or three-speed automatic
Capacity: 1,781cc
Bore and Stroke: 92 × 67mm
Maximum Speed: 199.6km/h (124mph)
Acceleration: 0–100km/h (0–60mph)＝9.5sec
Chassis: four-wheel drive. MacPherson struts on front suspension. Rear suspension by semi-trailing arms. Electronically controlled pneumatic springing
Dimensions: length 445cm (175.2in); width 168.9cm (66.5in)
Weight: 1,021.5–1,174.5kg (2,270–2,610lb)
Brakes: discs front and rear

The Subaru coupés are unashamedly unorthodox, and that is their main appeal. The external styling is unmistakeable, and the interior is equally idiosyncratic (the bizarre gear lever being a good example). Nevertheless, there is everything a modern sports coupé could need – four-wheel drive (developed from Subaru's simple off-road system), a healthy power output from its turbo engine, and even self-levelling dampers on its air-sprung strut front and semi-trailing rear arm suspension. That combination gives a good ride and handling that, with the four-wheel drive, provides brisk performance. However, what really sets the XT apart from the rest is that it dares to be different.

TOYOTA CELICA

Manufacturer: Toyota, Japan
Engine: four-cylinder 16-valve dual ohc; fuel-injected; (1.6lit) 124bhp at 6,600rpm, or (2.0lit) 150bhp at 6,400rpm, or (turbo) 182bhp at 6,000rpm
Gears: five-speed manual or four-speed automatic
Capacity: 1,587cc or 1,998cc
Bore and Stroke: 84×89mm
Maximum Speed: 199.6–220.6km/h (124–137mph)
Acceleration: 0–100km/h (0–60mph)=8.3sec (2.0lit), 7.9sec (turbo)
Chassis: front-wheel drive or four-wheel drive. Suspension by MacPherson struts front and rear. Also dual parallel lower links with anti-roll bar on the rear
Dimensions: length 436.6cm (171.9in); width 170.9cm (67.3in)
Weight: 108.25–1,417.5kg (2,405–3,150lb)
Brakes: ventilated discs front and rear
Steering: power-assisted rack and pinion

Japan has produced some outstanding machines in recent years, and the Toyota Celica holds a strong position in the 2-litre sports GT class. The basic Celica GT has good performance because of its 16-valve, 2-litre, fuel-injected engine which is complemented by an extremely efficient front-wheel-drive chassis.

The more powerful GT-Four variant, however, is the machine on which Toyota have based their attack on the World Rally Championship in the 1980s.

The GT-Four has a turbocharged engine producing 182bhp in road form and almost 500bhp in the rally cars. To exploit that power, it has a well-balanced, four-wheel drive chassis. This helps the car perform nearly as well in wet as in dry conditions.

TOYOTA MR2

For many years, the Bertone X1/9 dominated the mid-engined market, setting standards of handling unrivalled at the price. Then came the MR2 (which stands for Mid-engine, Rear-drive 2-seater), and by comparison the X1/9 seemed antiquated.

MacPherson strut suspension at the front and back allows comfortable suspension without compromising the sharp response which is the hallmark of a good mid-engined design. With 124bhp from just 1.6 litres, there is sufficient power for the driver to get the best from the MR2 on the twisting roads that are its true home. The addition of a mechanically driven supercharger has given even more power, but it is a moot point if the MR2 needs it.

Manufacturer: Toyota, Japan
Engine: four-cylinder; carburettor (1.4lit) 83bhp at 5,600rpm, or 16-valve dual ohc (1.6lit); fuel-injected; 124bhp at 6,600rpm, or supercharged 145bhp at 6,400rpm
Gears: five-speed manual or four-speed automatic
Capacity: 1,453cc, 1,587cc or 1,587cc supercharged
Bore and Stroke: 81 × 77mm
Maximum Speed: 196km/h (121.8mph)
Acceleration: 0–100km/h (0–60mph) = 8.0sec
Chassis: mid-engine rear-wheel drive. Suspension front and rear by MacPherson struts
Dimensions: length 394.9cm (155.5in); width 166.6cm (65.6in)
Weight: 951.75–1,111.5kg (2,115–2,470lb)
Brakes: discs front and rear
Steering: rack and pinion

TOYOTA SUPRA

Toyota have produced the Supra for those who require even more equipment and luxury than may be found in the Celica. There are two more cylinders, the Supra boasting a straight-six, 24-valve, twin-cam engine giving a displacement of 3 litres and an output of 204bhp.

The whole car is a showcase for high technology, containing Toyota's Acoustic Control Induction System to smooth low-speed running in the 24-valve cylinder head and also has knock sensors (unusual on a normally aspirated engine) to protect the engine. The Supra is luxurious and comfortable to drive and, thanks partly to its wishbone suspension, is able to cruise effortlessly for long distances at high speed.

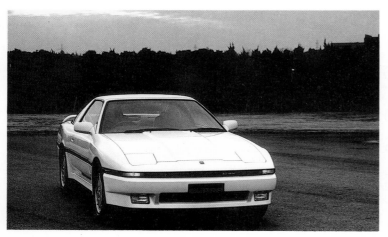

Manufacturer: Toyota, Japan
Engine: six-cylinder ohc; fuel-injected (2.0lit) 105bhp at 5,200rpm, or 24-valve dual ohc 140bhp at 6,200rpm, or turbo 185bhp at 6,200rpm, or 3.0lit 204bhp at 6,000rpm, or 3.0lit turbo 235bhp at 5,600rpm
Gears: five-speed manual or four-speed automatic
Capacity: 1,988cc or 2,954cc
Maximum Speed: 180.32–249.55km/h (112–155mph)
Acceleration: 0–100km/h (0–60mph)=7.9sec
Chassis: rear-wheel drive. Suspension by double wishbones front and rear.
Dimensions: length 463cm (182.3in); width 174.75cm (68.8in)
Weight: 1,289.25–1,539kg (2,865–3,420lb)
Brakes: discs front and rear with ABS

TVR have an excellent tradition of building very quick cars, and the 450 SEAC is currently one of the fastest British sports cars that money can buy.

Based on a heavily modified 4.5-litre (hence 450) Rover V8 engine, the SEAC (which is an acronym for Special Equipment Aramid Composite – referring to its construction from high-tech materials) has 320bhp at its disposal and a top speed of 266km/h (165mph).

The engine is not especially highly tuned but instead is a powerful motor which pulls hard throughout its rev range. The car's wide stance and short wheelbase make it nimble but tricky to handle at the limits of its performance – just like the illustrious Tuscan, which was TVR's outstanding sports car of the 1960s. But just like that old AC-Cobra-engined, bubble-backed coupé, the 450 SEAC has proved unbeatable in its class on the racetrack – as fine a testimony as one could wish for a sports car!

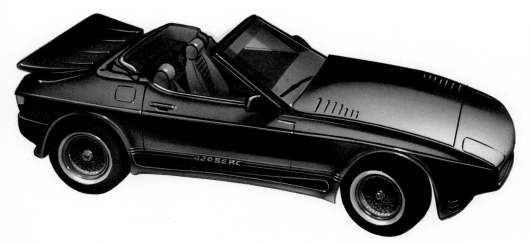

Manufacturer: TVR, Great Britain
Engine: V8 ohv; fuel-injected; 320bhp at 5,700rpm
Gears: five-speed manual
Capacity: 4,500cc
Bore and Stroke: 94 × 80mm
Maximum Speed: 265.7km/h (165mph)
Acceleration: 0–100km/h (0–60mph)=5.2sec
Chassis: rear-wheel drive. Kevlar reinforced body. Suspension by wishbones front and radius arms rear
Dimensions: length 408.43cm (160.6in); width 172.97cm (68.1in)
Weight: 1,140.75kg (2,535lb)
Brakes: discs front and rear
Steering: power-assisted rack and pinion

TVR S

TVR lost numerous customers when they decided to discontinue their classic sports cars with bubble rear windows in favour of the more angular and up-market Tasmin series, but the classically styled TVR is being manufactured again, albeit suitably modified to keep it competitive.

The TVR S is built around Ford's 2.9-litre V6 engine, which in its many forms has served TVR well over the years. The V6 is installed in a tubular chassis which is then clothed in a glassfibre body. Like the rest of its stablemates, the TVR S has an ingenious hood with a fold-up rear section. As this is braced into place by struts, the frame secures two roof panels to the screen surround. These panels are tailored by teams of craftsmen to each individual car.

Manufacturer: TVR, Great Britain
Engine: V6 ohv; fuel-injected; 168bhp at 6,000rpm
Gears: five-speed manual
Capacity: 2,933cc
Bore and Stroke: 93 × 72mm
Maximum Speed: 225.4km/h (140mph)
Acceleration: 0–100km/h (0–60mph) = 7.0sec
Chassis: rear-wheel drive. Epoxy-coated steel chassis with one piece glassfibre-reinforced body. Front suspension by wishbones. Rear suspension by semi-trailing arms
Dimensions: length 400cm (157.5in); width 145cm (57.1in)
Weight: 940kg (2,072lb)
Brakes: front discs and rear drums
Steering: rack and pinion
Notes: uses Ford engine.